The Voice in the Wood

Selected Poetry

Barry Middleton

Ah, when to the heart of man
was it ever less than a treason
to go with the drift of things,
to yield with a grace to reason,
and bow and accept the end
of a love or a season?
　　　　　　　　　　Robert Frost

Author's Note

The easiest part of putting together a collection of poetry is deciding what not to include. Of course a declaration such as this opens the door to criticism as the implication is that these poems represent my best work. But the critic would be missing the point. Basically, these are just poems that I like, it's that simple.

Most of these verses were written while I was between the ages of twenty and thirty. As such, I could excuse some of them as products of the excessive emotion of youth. I could, but I will not since advancing age has chosen not to spare me those same excesses. The more recent work, I would hope, contains the same naive passion as the poems from my youth.

Poetry is about birth and death and what comes between. It is not a study of literature nor has it anything to do with fashion. Poetry is a portrait of feelings, success and failure and lessons learned or not. It is about rebirth, new attempts, new beginnings, love, joy, tears and unrequited dreams.

To include or not include some love poems was my biggest dilemma. But I finally decided that love is too important a part of life to omit. Other poems are lessons from childhood and from young adulthood. It was those times that formed my character and my belief. Some of the poems were written recently. I will leave it to you to figure out which ones.

I hope the reader will find here what I felt in the writing - the surprise, the joy, the fear, the pain and the occasional ecstasy of living.

Memories of the Seasons

On a Florida summer afternoon,
I try to bring inside the heat
of soupy air I work through tired lungs.
My air is a studied breath,
is inspiration to unravel
the tired knots of memory.
Breath,
the lifetime poem,
comes to this,
the hot and the cold,
the bright and the dark,
the wet and the dry.
It is easy to think of extremes
in Florida.
I work to breathe
as beads of sweat condense
on forehead and neck
and beads of memory drip
like water drops
from my exhausted air conditioner.
The waters grow memories
of hot and cold,
of birth and death,
of love and loss.
The heat reminds me
of the heat of long ago
and strangely of the cold to come.
The heat reminds me
I am alive on borrowed time.
I remember the childish heat

of August at home in Mississippi,
and the weary heat
of sixty beloved summers.
In a nearby oak
a cousin of a remembered squirrel
lies flat on a limb
and pants to cool its small brain
and dreams of fall and fat acorns
while I fight for air to fuel a few more
memories of the seasons.

Sonnet of Spring

Not to spring only is the sun confined
but in the dreadful winter, dread removes.
It leaves a lacy pattern so refined
upon the snow and thus approves.
As when it passes into night,
from sight it dies,
but dusk belies
when plainly moon and stars reflect its might.
Nor only at zenith is felt the light,
or early the morning,
or late the evening,
but through our days and into night.
    Not to spring only is the sun confined,
    it leaves a lacy pattern so refined.

Ending

If when I die I stop
to tally the score,
I pray that tears will cease
and memory's smile
and laughter
will soften the death rattle.

Recollection is fleeting
like the green flash
of a Florida sunset.
I want to waken
sunny days
and how the rain
brought wild flowers.

The greatest gift
an old man has
is afterthought.
If life rushes
before my eyes
as the sun sets,
let it flash the pleasures
I have known
like a manic slide show
of hot green summers.

If memory captures
life and death,
I will recall it all
when I am old

and live my life again
passing over loving sunsets,
smiling children,
and gentle moments
to die in the arms
of my mother
and death
will never be a deceit.

Sonnet 37

Love goes as love grows
like polliwogs to frogs
whose wiggliness no longer shows
in leaping out from logs.
Love's occult when love's adult
and somber in her days,
and makes no effort to rebut
her oriental ways.
Love's at rest when love is best,
when passion's bit is done,
then love settles on her nest
and contemplates the sun.
Love's a gaudy lily
in the first days of May,
a wildflower memory
on a cold December day.

Early Seeding

Before the spring,
before the bare twigs
of my season tree
began to show
a damp green haze
within their brittle net,
I caught one day a neighbor
out with hoe and spade
to turn the earth
and seed an early garden.
I did not think it bold to ask,
since the old man was of an age
too near eternal mystery
to hide the little that he knew.
He saw the question coming
because I asked with the eyes
before I asked straight out.
"Early for a garden ain't it?"
He didn't stop to clean his spade.
He knew exactly what he'd say
and looked to see if I was set to hear.
An early spring would come
was all he said.
I wanted something more profound
and kept him on the hook.
"What if spring is late
and your work's undone
by late frost?" I asked.
"Suppose it is," he said
and sunk his spade again.

Sonnet 39

The only picture on the wall
reminds me of a love I had,
two dancers frozen to recall
a love the painter once had known.
He holds her in his arms as if
to say that love is always new.
Now time has passed, its only gift,
a brief, translucent shade of blue.
So love and friends too quickly pass
as sun beats down and pictures fade.
So life assumes an azure shade,
as suns go down and yesterdays
begin to subtly change their hue
to brief, translucent shades of blue.

Relativity

Poetry is tangential.
It does not follow life
like a faithful dog.
Poetry is thought at
escape velocity.
The appearance is
rising above.
The reality is
breaking away.

Recycle

Lonely rivers do not grieve
but flow to mother sea.
The lonely life that I must leave
conspires to set me free.

The river passes by a brook
and takes its living there
and does not lend a backward look
and has no sense to care.

A river and a man are one
and go the way they must.
When eulogy is said and done
the waters are a trust.

A borrowed soul will bless the sand
collected at the sea;
the skeletal remains of man
are setting fishes free.

Sonnet 46

My window in the night that lets in stars
is there for me to open and recall
that though I live within a frightened wall,
fear, like windows, can be set ajar.

Walls are built by men who understand
the complex laws of fear and bravery,
the intermix of will and slavery,
nature's strength in alms or in demand.

This ancient wall is built of solid stone;
it closes in the soul and blocks the view.
A window takes me places never gone,
the freedom of the stars in evening hue.

A window open to the night and fearless
gathers stars to give new strength to weariness.

Incidentals here in us
are instrumental to the thrush.
                                        1969

Instrumentals to a man
are incidental to the plan.
                                        1976

Beginning

The ritual
of hopefulness
is always the same.
Velvet night
is a soft vibration
as my eyes meet hers,
with curiosity
and fantasies
of what might be.
Later,
talking,
feeling,
the thread is spun
that wraps us in each other
like a thing hoping to happen.
Plastic gestures cease.
Again there is a breathing thing,
alive like the evening air,
a darting thing like eyes meeting,
a tentative thing,
a blessing,
a possibility.

Grassy Key Deer

Down the beach
was rocky coral,
split,
bleached,
and tossed
by a million
sighs of the sea.
Once wet,
living
and brilliant
with color,
now laced with debris,
dead remnants
of used up existence,
rusted skeletons,
salt white bone.
Heading back
a key deer I saw
fantastic and dainty
failed to notice
the fatal metaphor
and ate
the remaining grass.

The Cynic

Life is filled with honest men breeding disaster
from simple solutions and good intentions.

Love is a hasty decision based on limited
evidence and extremely poor advice.

Children are the means by which mistakes
are passed from one generation to the next.

Three Nieces Watch a Scary Movie

three
blond and delicate
in chocolate faces
hands on lips
watching the imaginary
disaster
wide eyes
trembling and delicious

Key West Madonna

The girl in blue upon the sand
intrigues me like this southern land.
She always smiles as if to say
that I should speak, but not today.

She watches casually her child
and notices my sometimes smile,
then turns to check and be assured
to find her view is not obscured
but playing idly on the sand,
a tiny shell held tight in hand.

I watched her from the farther side
struck dumb before the southern tide
and might have spoke to only say
that she was beautiful today.

But to the sea beneath the foam
I nourished other thoughts of home,
a longing to be small and free -
the tide lets go and leaves me be.

Three Verses on Rhythm

Did witches meet a summer night
for rhythmic chants and easy rest
and were they at their very best
envisioning the sight?
A wanderer in a foreign land,
weakly natal, blinding sand
and salty kicks while in the spell
and dreamy drifts between the swells.
Then mingling love and lust with dew,
a prayer, a chant, a fork of yew,
begat a creature wholly new.
On summer nights the coven meets,
a cauldron for a sea,
to make a potion somnolescent
and rock you in the moon's new crescent.

I looked into the sky a summer
Sunday afternoon
and breathed the air
and thought I saw the rhythm of a wave.

The gray solitude of spring overtakes me,
as a storm washes out slowly,
intensities of hue.
I do not know the truth, the lie,
immensities forsake me.
Youth is wise to
ponder, not too long,
the meaning of a rhythm,
the nuance of a song.

The City

Great slabs
are laid into her maw
like ribbons of death
tied neatly with a concrete bow.
She ruminates on robot wheels,
humanity reduced to steel.
Within her entrails the slow
mutation of a nation breeds.
Is this the unction of man's pity?
The obesity of a city.

Exhaustion

I am exhausted
the party has gone on
too long
and still the guests
linger
like the last leaves
of autumn
defiant against the night
or merely fearing sleep
they gesture against the
chill of evening

The Greenhouse at Leu Gardens

When winter gloom is all my view
and days like harvest fruit
weigh heavy on a weathered frame
too weak for such a load,
then I know a place to go
where, domiciled as warm as June,
secret orchids fuel a passion fire
and fragrant walls in tropic bloom
reflect the damp of loving August nights.
The colors there are set among the green
like Genesis in rhyme.
Saurian fern and cycads grow
below an ancient roof
now glazed with primal moss.
Yet I feel these panes of grizzly glass
are facets in a rare gem,
the ransom for broken winter moods
till the season yields.

Time Piece

Now as the clock arms
fall toward dawn,
I lie alone but not alone.

My brain ticks like clock springs
straining to unwind the day.

And by my side you lay
tricking dreams, electric ticks.

And so two brains uncoil,
two brains, one sleeps,
the other silently toils.

Death

In a dream came a stranger
all in black and smiling.
And foolish trust compelled me
and I said enter friend
and did not turn to see
but only heard
the whistle of the scythe.

Winter Stand

Have I known winter but a day?
I shudder if I have a way
to go before the warm lets down
her sunbeams on a frozen town.

Like men on winter walks who ask,
"How long before the hill is past?"
I long for easy slope to home
but climb the seeker's way, alone.

I should have known to listen to reason
and bundle for a harder season.
I should have gone out with a friend
that we could joke about the wind.

Oh when does man suffer defeat
when well prepared and on his feet?
It makes me want to lay a plan
and take a grander winter stand.

Supernova

To know that death will come to all
should be a consolation to the seasons,
that nature too must deign to fall
at random and bereft of reasons.

For like a man, the sun will dim,
and should some balding progeny
control that day,
observe the protestation,
I think that he alone might see
the mote of man's divinity.

When all the suns explode
and god doth laugh
uproarious in her cave,
the slave will turn to welcome death,
the King will have no grave.

Sun Course

The sun props up an elbow in the dawn
and casts a sleepy yawn,
inquisitive birds to test the air.
They travel with the leaves, a wave
of dreams transported by a primal breath.

The sun stands upright, the heat of noon
emanates a grating order
that makes the humble beasts
stampede among the scrub, nightmare-like,
fleeing prima facie rule.

The sun then sets in the ancient west,
soft shadow sounds remain
of rustling sheets as wise animals
glide among the palms that edge the sea,
like death seeking out its source.

The Final Piece

You have watched me when I wept
and kissed my silent eyes in sleep
and I have set my secrets free,
you know what is to know of me.

And what I lost or what I gave
concerns me not at all tonight
but was love just too much to bear
or not enough to even care?

I'd sleep the better if I knew,
was it in me or was it you?
How does a parting come to pass
when lovers swear that love will last
and believe it so they do not hide
one clue to solve this ancient riddle?

Domestic

the wife of the artist walked in
apologetically
her eyes would not have wept
had she known
he made paintings
by instinct
but she made love
by inspiration

Values

the silent perfection
of the wilderness
makes no boasts
the song of the dead poet
has no pretense
and there is a value too
in the gray of the winter sky
when the color of the sky
and sea are one

love leaves in autumn
for we would not have her go
amid lilies and unaware of the cold

when they kissed
the world was out of balance
denied its centricity
it wobbled drunkly
through the night
and though she cried
god puts none aside
to puzzle out the plan

when all the prayers were done
the silent shadow of a nun
beckoned him to gently come
and view a second of the past
that must forever last
a glimpse of chicken bones and ash
that vanish in a flash - that vanish...

in the gray light of tomorrow
a soldier dies
for distant daylight
mother's cries
and though the dress
is neatly tied
no blush will fall
upon the bride

Adrian Hammer didn't know
the use of any winter snow
or why the world must move so slow
with large investments in the town
his stocks were up and never down
he believed that what he'd lost was found
in his respect the county round
he did not die a flashy death
but old and tired just went to rest
his friends all thought it for the best

the mud upon my shoes
becomes the life
upon my age
if I look closely
and remember
I will behold
no plan I have begun
and no regret
that did not hold me
in the passion of life

The Empty Journal

an abandoned smokehouse on the home place
whose smoky fires had long grown cold
was a storehouse for broken dreams
forgotten memories
and blond fantasies of times past

we used the place to play our children's games
when old ones rocked the porch and paced the day
like molasses from the mule turned cane mill
down by the pond
we invented mysteries there when none presented

I recall I went there all alone on a romantic day
and found discarded in a tray of family treasure
my favorite book
I opened it and took a look

it was an empty diary
a journal that the lady of the house
intended always to begin and end
but never found the time to write an idle line

there were too many meals to cook
too many clothes to wash
too many times the rains were slight
or just as bad a flood
times when her only plans
were to bolster her husband's
against both their doubts

and yet he died
then she
the book was set aside untouched
my favorite
leaving me to put upon its empty face
what I would
love
death
an embrace

Failure to Site Scripture

To make you laugh
and cry at once
was never my plan,
was only a hunch
I played in the sand.
You see,
I was walking the beach alone
without an example in paper or stone
of how life is ample
and amply provides
for laughter and tears
and feelings we hide.

The Old Road

Behind the farm in an ancient wood
an ancient road followed the ridge
like I followed the tread of my father,
trying to make my steps as big as his.
The road had more success I'd say,
for it was carved from wilderness
in days when no machine
could flatten hill nor fill a hollow
so boys could find no spot along the way
to race a scooter in a trial of honor.
The road was walled where mules
had cut a trace, though not so deep
there was not still a hill to quicken
our walk or slow it to a turtle pace.
The way was vaulted there with trees.
It was a sacred place to pause,
to pray,
to play,
to wonder
if by chance some Confederate miser
had buried gold
as the story we were told.
The road had been there long
before the land divided North
and South in war.
And farther up the way there stood
in a meadow in the wood
an old piano church of African race.
There was no song upon its face,
its eyes had long been boarded shut,

the churchyard path was now a rut.
But nothing along the old road
could hold me in its vines embrace for long
save a simple house too abandoned
for even the poorest sharecropper
to wish it his. When first I came
to its door it had contents,
broken furniture and other remnants
of the former tenants.
The only thing that stayed there then
was truly not alive -
a fantasy of broken dreams,
evil mysteries and ghosts.
They made me run through thickets
propelled by common sense
and back to the church
for self defense.
But I was just a child
playing in the wood
and now not one sight along
the way is left unchanged
but the road itself.
Whatever stayed upon that hill
has left me to haunt another childhood.
Now the only fears that haunt
are phantom deeds of living men
that make me want to dream
a childhood dream again.

On Leaning Left

I watch the children walk the garden wall.
They step too slow and then must step too fast
to keep from falling on the walk or grass.
They lean to left to keep from falling right.
They lean the other way to compensate for sway.
I wonder if they know the game they play
with eyes so fixed upon their nearest step.
More than one I saw that day so studied
his last move he missed the corner turn
and so he fell and bruised a knee.
I wondered why the tears
for I was old enough to see
one faulty step was cause enough
to set the others free.

Thoughts

Love is very like ideas,
not always there
when you need it.
Hope is sustained
by its own
peculiar
lack of logic.

Jones' Situation

halfway to the one legged man
with rotund posterior
spring said nothing to Simon Jones
only instinct repeated and repeated
the scarcity of birds
the thin guise of civilization
shrubs trimmed neatly
in a vain attempt to hide
the pagan voodoo symbols
selected for wholeness
Simon knew only hungry people
and some that eat
Simon prayed often
and washed his hands
and showed his poems
to close friends
and in the end
sold all he had
and moved to the tropics

Time

Time is the cruelest element,
passing slowest in misery
and swiftest in joy.

Time,
god's silent toy,
takes a little
of what is valued most
and
takes a little more,
un-noticed
as we assume to outwit death.

Time gets even with men
who pay it little heed.

Taken for granted
and hating life
it knifes out
its piece of flesh.

Swift knife in pain,
slow in healing
and yet
so greedily appealing.

Gift

You gave as the rain gives,
enduring through the living months,
and more
as seeds spring out a memory.
No price repays the cloud,
it becomes the earth,
a flower,
life.

Tiger Eye

I looked into the tiger's eye
and shared the air
that only fools
would dare to breathe.
I heard my heart above the beast
but with the beast
and in the beast.
I looked into the tiger's eye
and saw my empty stare.

D.E.

As near as I could tell
with youthful wisdom,
men fear two things.
First there are other men,
and probably could be first,
unavoidable circumstance.
D.E. was both in childhood days,
a man and yet a colder thing,
a symbol of evil in a blond world,
a lesson that there are things unknown
and better left un-investigated.
My older brother found the knife
back near the backside of our property.
Not an old and rusty tool,
no mind you,
but only tinged by one day's dew,
a hot trail.
On its pearly side a diamond plaque
was double traced and within that tracing
an enigmatic inscription was engraved,
the letters D.E.
A man,
an unknown intruder into our lives,
defiled our tabernacle,
came into our sacred woods
where each hill and hammock
had a holy name and almost every tree.
He had come in darkness,
alone and demon-like,
carrying a rude weapon

snatched from his hand
by guardian angelic forces.
His intent could not have been good.
And so,
whenever a voice came through the wood,
we ran.
The world was no longer safe
with a man like this on the place
consorting with the devil.
There was no defense
against this profanation.
We knew he held an evil power
and though months would pass
without a broken twig or footprint
to speak of his presence,
it was always there.
We knew he might step forth
at any moment
from the bowels
of some great, hollow beech
and take us in our innocence.
We would never forget
the unseen terror
of his circumstance
and my father
would always
keep the knife.

Butterfly Girl

love is like a butterfly
with little boys a running
nets in hand they flutter by
and think that they're just funning
alighting on a puggy nose
or tripping on some dainty toes
you'd think that little boys would know
that little girls are cunning

Hot Dogs and Champaign

I did not soon sleep immune
from your caress
and what you saw of desire
and uncertainty
may have kept you waking also
had you known
how touch can spare
a longer sleep

Youth on the Wing

All little girls just have to know
the whys of life and how things go,
like why it is that birds must sing
and why the flowers bloom in spring.

Their mothers grow accustomed
to the questions that they ask,
but when they come and question you,
you know it's quite some task.

It's like the child I see today,
a fragile bird in every way,
who lately ruffles my surprise
and looks me straight into the eyes.

"Is there a place for everything?"
she murmurs like a dove.
"Tell me father, if you know,
where do they keep the love?"

Feline

Go slowly like a cat
that flirts and rubs
and sits upon my lap
then purrs without delay
the first sign of day.
Curl up upon my bed
and touch me with a paw
and stretch a feline limb
without a flaw.
Go slowly like a cat,
and cunning
with my love.
That sound is but
a night bird's call
and all your stalking time
is free,
tonight the only prey
is me.

Cold

Life proves that loss
is never worth the cost.
Every man discovers
that something in life
knows the northern side.

The County Fair

When I was just a hometown kid
the county fair came round each fall
and I would ride the easy rides
and wonder what went on inside
the tent down near the end where men
would gather like chickens after corn.
I'd ride the easy rides and stay
within my brother's call as I
was told to do. It took me years
to deem myself a man and dare
to lift the musty skirt of that
remotest tent and swagger to
the ticket booth of deadly fun.
But how the thing did climb and dive,
it made me appreciate being alive.
And the girls in the corner tent?
Why they were that much better,
my eyes were that much older,
my eyes were that much wetter.

Going On

Just passing through on the way to life
I have not often encountered belief.
No, only twice I can recall,
once in the spring and once in fall.

The Fort

It was our multi-purpose shack,
the playhouse of my early youth.
The fort was a place
to carry out childish experiments
and a place to hide
from the secret torments
of growing up.
There was chemistry there,
old fashioned bottles
that once held pills and potions.
Green ones, blue, brown and clear,
some were oddly shaped,
the trademark of a mighty tonic.
There was protection there,
a door to close
against the tyranny of schoolwork
and chores and worry.
The fort smelled of the earth
that was its foundation.
I learned there
about the solubility
of talcum powder,
about brotherhood
and what it feels like
to pause a while
and wonder
and pretend.

The Tree House

The ceremonial main beam
went up in spring,
an oak two by six
so heavy it took
us all together with our mother
to hold it up while I bent nails
against its obstinate solidity.
The pyramids
must have been easier to build.
Boards were brought
from every scrap pile
on the place and we would
make a production with
the addition of each one
and raise them with a block
and tackle as if we were
dedicating some monument
to time.
The construction of the tree house
took till summer,
the landscaping went on till fall
in Shady Valley
and there was a permanent position
for someone willing to work,
maintenance of the kitty cat cemetery,
also the resting place of rabbits, dogs
and a two headed turtle.
And there was a bridge to be built;
there is always a bridge to be built.

Resignation

On the edge of a cliff,
on the edge of a night,
a dark little cabin
is edged by my light.

So close to the edge
of destruction it stood
that I feared that my light
might do it no good
but tumble it headlong
with splintering wood
down rocks to the river
and end it for good.

And I wondered a man
should pick such a site
to lay his head down
for even a night.

But the storm at my back
convinced me to stay,
to die in the night
if death had its way.

Heat

coldness
meet the tropic wind
you have sought
across a continent
you are spent
and the sun
will burn

September Wine

If I were forced to make a brief summation
of what was worth the time and what was not,
I would not go the way of some I've seen
and trace the river to its source and stop
my finger on each town where I found joy.
That takes too long and I haven't the time.
I'll give the best example I can find
and offer you a cup of Autumn wine.
The latest thing I loved was just a girl,
there's no grand statement there, no distant pearl
of wisdom there to keep you sane or add
a lot to the common store of philosophy.
Love is like youth, like gold it cannot stay,
yet now I'd give it all for just a day.
But if you ask advice for those in love,
I'd tell them, "Love, but always keep in mind
the time may come to drink September wine."

Love Poem

Dawn's music,
secrets,
and the damp air
of early morning,
are things progressively
more melancholy.
Until like the music,
like the heavy air,
like the secrets
and warm feelings,
we are part of the air,
part of the music,
making secrets
in the closeness
of sunrise.

Dawn Leaves

love does not leave without the dawn
it takes the early morning light away
and leaves us only with the day
the days are easy to endure
the nights are filled with single sighs
and fear the sun will never rise
the sun is high when I awake
love does not leave without the dawn
for sleepless nights
are blind to eastern light

Mobile Bay 1964

It was not necessary
for the two of us to shout
above the roar of the boat's motor,
white foam behind us
and black water night all around.

We were thankful for the
red and green lights on the buoys
and far away
a line of yellow dots
encircled us
and put an edge to eternity.

When we jumped the wake
of an inbound freighter
our hearts dropped a beat.

Then we heard the dredges drumming
where men worked through the night
to let us know the world was alive.

Satartia - Clear Lake Camp - 1967

A gray wooden skiff
is moored in ink black water,
water as dark as the midnight sky
miles from town.
Floating autumn leaves
and green gold duckweed
move along the surface
like a liquid forest
in a quiet breeze.
Moving in stillness,
the water inches its way
parabolically
past a rustic cabin.
Odors of leaves, fish
and stove smoke
breathe life
to the cool clean air.
Game taste, evening,
and a toast to friendship,
bring a sleep like peacefulness
as forest animals find their beds.
Oak, tupelo and cypress pillars
sweep skyward
from land and half-land wetness
and diffuse into a pediment
of green and bronze and indigo.
The setting sun glows red hot steel
across the waters of the slough
and mirrors all.
I see myself there still,

sitting solemn and silent
like a benevolent god
meting out providence
to the creation he loves.

Chain Gang Mississippi 1965

I watched over Ceasollie
in convict stripes
as he worked the road
and sang his songs
soft and meek and beautiful.

I watched him by day
and I drank quietly at home
as careful white men do
and never stood on tables
nor sang in all night cafes.

I watched over Ceasollie
in jail for being poor
and boisterous
and black.

The Introvert

The walks I used to take at home
in Mississippi told me more
I think of men and such than all
the chatter of the lecture hall.
My eyes would move from tree to tree
and see a man in every trunk.
I met the extroverted oak
and thought he did not care for what
I said. He had the brawn to stand
a storm; his roots meandered far
and wide. I said he touched the Earth
too light that way. His pride in such
an insubstantial stay was sure
to be his downfall if indeed
he would not set a deeper tap.
But then my eyes engaged near by
a shattered introverted pine.

Silence Sleeps

When silence sleeps
exhausted
in the dead of night,
then watchers
turn their heads
and night sounds
come to life.
Not heard before
while silence watched,
the murmur of the city,
the whisper of a garden,
a lover's breath,
is heard the louder
that she sleeps
till droning
in the morning light
she raises sleepy arms
and sweeps away the noise
before the children wake.

Self Defense - A Song

No, honestly officer
I didn't say fuzz;
I'm just headed for home
to cop a good buzz
and I don't see the harm,
if harm me it do,
it only hurts me
it doesn't hurt you.
If I did a crime
it's one that can save me
from doing much worse
it helps to behave me
and keep me off streets
in the dead of the night
and out of big trouble
and out of big fights.
Now I fight with myself
and what's on my mind
and it gives me a tool
and it gives me some time.
So, honestly officer
I didn't say fuzz;
I'm just headed for home
to cop a good buzz
and I don't see the harm,
if harm me it do,
it only hurts me
it doesn't hurt you.
It doesn't hurt you!

Accumulated Defense

The fire has fallen on itself,
the earth beneath my back is cold.
I could get up to build some heat,
a firm foundation still remains
in coals that glow with ghostly flames.
Yet I have been alone too long
to ever believe a midnight fire
could compensate for what is lost,
my only warmth against the frost
that I have gathered to my bed
like one in unfamiliar woods
gone out to initiate the spring.
I've had a little bit of good
I gathered to myself for wood
and if a shoulder grows too chill
I know life means me no great ill
and no one is here to get alarmed
if my cold I turn onto my warm
and my warm I turn to heat the storm.

The Children Play

the children play
in the aftermath of summer

heat and dust are memories
the opulence of water has vanished

green leaves and iced tea
steaming air
has given up
to warm meals
falling leaves
and stove smoke

autumn is not sad
autumn is an infant season
that looks toward joyful snow
good books
warm fires
and peaceful sleep

the children play
in the aftermath of summer

Long Lesson

Some man's future lover
in undone pigtail curls
and out to walk her brother
in the world of little girls
came down the walk and singing,
not what the world was bringing,
but carefree childish songs
that did not say how long
the lesson for today
would take to have its say.
A boy and girl together
to test the springtime weather
in innocence and play
will come another day
and others without end
to try and understand
whatever love demands.
The little boy, whose heart
will break before he calls
himself a man, the girl,
who trades her youth for love,
her life in growing closer
to that which birth denied her,
the other one beside her.

Fruit Fly

A greenish fly with golden eyes
did chance to interrupt my sighs
then buzzed away to investigate
what next would prove to be its fate.

I let him bite and rub a wing
and thought how life's a fragile thing
involving little bits of good
that cannot last like wishes would.

And I continued to contemplate
this curious creature that came of late
to use a precious piece of life
to see if I was food or strife
or something that could be of use
to a fly's short life of mild abuse.

And I do not think it all for naught
that he got but a single grain of salt.

Rubric

He is like an actor
grown tired
of monologues,
tired of attacking truth
by indirection,
love by innuendo.

Truth,
he says,
is but a temporary agreement,
a Rube Goldberg
that accomplishes its end
by indiscreet complaint
and within restraints.

Love?
Not even that!
The ball rolls off
the ramp,
in the wrong
direction.

Mississippi Mercy   - Vicksburg

You can't convince me living in the town
with all its air pollution, dirt and crime,
is harder on the health than country style.
Sickness is a country way of life;
that's the way it always was and is.
A visit home is a visit to The Home;
that's what I think of country hospitals,
the major illness there being just old age.
Along the way the countryside is green.
If grace were green one might conclude that God
so pitied Mississippi that he spilled
his richest portion on the sickly land
to compensate the farmer's plight of toil.
I pass by palmist Sister Kane's estate,
a shack behind a sign and sunken gate,
the sign of Christ in Christian day glow red
and dripping paint for blood into a palm.
Inside the T.V. set is tuned to Him
who gave his life to pay the rent for them.
I ask directions at the local Shell.
I want to ask the rednecks, "Were is Mercy?"
But I know they wouldn't get my city play.
They tell me how to find the hospital
returning to their beer and talk of fish.
Strange apostles lead me now-a-days,
"Just take a left on Grove and go-a-ways."

The Good Doctor

I place a bet that he would call at home
like country doctors laid beneath their stone,
interred beneath the earth of all their cures
to rest a while at last. If heaven lures
the kind and patient soul, informed but never
proud, I think that God could speak aloud
and praise that rare compassion in a man
that never chides but always lends a hand.
I'd like to thank him for the work he did
but we are taught to be impersonal,
withholding praise from those deserving it,
like western love, restrained and always fit
for viewing by the very young. But I
refuse to believe that God intended that,
for love is just the better part of God,
the part he left for us to know; and praise
is virtues just reward that through our days
reminds us of a better time to come
when all our cares and worries are undone.
Those country doctors rest in heaven's heart
and wait for him to come and take his part.

Come Up to Dawn

Come up to dawn with me and bed
and sooth my reeling somber head.
I would forsake all memory
to know our night time ecstasy.
The plaster room will turn to gold
if you are shy and I am bold.
We will not speak deceiving words
but hear instead the dawning birds
who take our part and fears away
as we make love to greet the day.

Solitary Concert

Outside the imprisoned symphony,
violins right and woodwinds left,
past the books and French doors,
the painted landscape waits
for you to make it sing.

The night, with all its
daylight hidden noise,
I shut outside
for sadder sounds
of emptiness,
of voiceless walls
that echo with the sound
of only music.

Lost Music

I never heard a song till you
came down to lay with me
and all of life I thought was mute,
the flowers in the park
began to tremble in the dark
and tune themselves for me.

    I never thought that words had breath
    but those you spoke to me
    still linger in my memory
    and nightly breathe a sigh
    which says that love should never die.

I never knew what silence was
till silent in my room
I reached for you and found you gone
and lost your haunting tune.

Acceptance

The morning came up
in beautiful exhaustion,
a silver fog drifted across
the cool green valley.

Birds sang that life had just begun,
the flutes were playing low.

So human it is to want more,
the curse of intellect.

The apes were happy
hunting riper fruit,
finding Darwin.

Let tired old morning
be our teacher.
Want, but hold heaven.

Notion

I don't know where I got the notion,
perhaps while swimming in the ocean,
that human life is minnow frail
besides the deep domain of whale.

But once while sunning on the land
I thought I had the plot in hand
that men are gods and we had won.
I'd stayed too long beneath the sun.

For soon the land returns to sea.
Will death return heaven to me?

Is God locked up within my heart
or does He die as minnows dart
and flee the greater natural force
of sharks as preternatural source.

Brain Damage

Love went out like satin night
unnoticed in narcotic dreams.
Love left me doped like a clay star,
like a cushion made of stone.

Satin, soft one,
your eyes were wet as birth
and exactly brown.

My hangover is gone
like silk opium into the worm.

It hurt me more to lose my mind
than to lose you.

And yet, my granite sobriety,
asylum gray,
whispers nightly excuses
of how I want to love you
in old, hypnotic dreams
and laced with the softness
of a tender, breathless embrace.

A Child

wanderer of blue eyes
and silver seeking hair
following a white moth
you will not wonder long
why white wings transform
to green leaves and orange fruit
in a twinkling as the wind shifts
you want neither intoxicant
nor philosophy
nor squirming guesses
but turning your head
to your smiling mother
you laugh
and scan the grass
for newness

Confrontation

I wander far to seek and think
and rarely find the answer I
was looking for, but often delve
another just as needful of
solution. I recall a day
I thought that man endured above
the whole of Earth in beast or plant.
My walk that day did chance upon
a hummingbird out sipping blooms
of golden yellow honeysuckle.
I thought: here are the frailest things
that God has given roots or wings
and yet they have endured not knowing
love or hate and feeling no
regret if we had never met.
I was as frail as they I knew
and not the stronger for a brain
but likely weaker for the pain
that I could feel that they could not.

Dream

I stole a little piece of day
the world was sleeping through
to watch a mist of fog transform
my neighbor's lawn to fantasy.

I heard the dawn's enchanted
birds, sweet cantations
to pass the spell along,
the dream we claim is real.

The blackened sky
turns nearly white
before the baby blue
and girlish pink
gives up to surer blue
and time to think.

How hard it is
for me to hold
a sorrow in the dawn,
for dawn is a mirage
of what might be.

And yet how easy
it can be
to forsake hope,
to nourish a sorrow
with the chimera
of yesterday.

The Gravedigger

I was no philosopher
and not the master gravedigger;
I took no pride and did not
understand the job I did.
Old Craig, the lazy digger,
gave advice and laid it out.
And Hubert, the artist of the crew,
would take a sharpened spade
to even up the sides and make
them true. Howard and I,
or brawn and useless intellect,
would throw the slack from
out the hole and cut a
little deeper down till we
were told to stop.
I did not understand the fuss
and careful contemplation
of the pit, not as long as the
coffin fit. But I was just
eighteen, too young to realize
that this was art, the final
mark a man would cause
upon the earth, the ditch
unlike the others that would
be re-dug and altered
by the years and whims
of other workers. No, this
was permanent work for
pay, the likes of which
is hard to find today.

A Fisherman's Prayer

I feel I've been out fishing fifty years
and just as leave would call it quits for now
and throw the whole catch back for other men
to cast their lines upon and dream their dreams.

I've searched and thought the waters far from home
and tried to calculate what waits for me
before the liquid future takes me in,
the stream of life that sweeps me toward the tomb.

And I would pull my anchor for one wish
and free the living and the dead alike
if I could catch what hides behind a bend,
what might well be as fishermen pretend.

Above Despair

I wish to die in day old love
like leaving work on a good Friday,
in a good week, in a good year.

I want to never crest the hill
but dream the landscape there
for disappointing heights I've topped.

I want to die painting a hope
on a rare old rainy day
when light is all within.

I pray that gods, or law of odds
will choose a time above despair
for no dread scythe must find me there.

A Common Situation

The shadow that love cast
upon my recent past
will die at evening's end
and then I'll comprehend
that night is for the best
that puts shadows to rest.

It is a lonely night
without a sign of light
that puts an end to love,
that seems an endless grove
in some enchanted wood
of deep and somber mood.

Yet night gives way to dawn
and wood gives out to lawn
and hurt gives in to heal.

The essence of the deal
is not mistaking night
for some uncommon plight.

Friend

You are my friend.
In my home
you may come as you are
and stay as you like.

There is nothing that is mine
and mine alone
that you may not share.

You owe me nothing
for this fragile gift,
but put your joy
for my reward
in giving you
that opposite
of loneliness
we call
friendship.

Twilight's Tow

It's been a while
since I have watched
the evening settle in and fill
the silence up with blackness.
It comes the same however;
too long I've stayed outdoors.
I turn and watch my shadow
reaching out toward night
that silent, pours through trees
a mile away. My homeward
walk will find me in the dark
before the backyard gate swings to
and startled dogs begin to bark.
A thousand limbs
that scraped my face
and just as many spider webs
I failed to see, you'd think
should make me watch the time.
But twilight's steady tow,
however rare it may have been,
will find a mind with too much on it
and holds me in the growing dark
to tally up the worth today
of what was done
and what was yet to do.

Dusty Floors and Open Windows

I miss the days
of childhood dreams,
of innocence in flowers,
childish games,
dusty floors
and open windows.

Another country boy has come to town.
I know him by the soup bowl cut
and nervous way he counts my change.

In the midst of the latest deal,
I grow tired,
feeling I've fumbled the words.

I recall a simple stream
and a modest child,
a frame farmhouse,
the smell of spring
and dusty floors
and open windows.

Interfacial

The grass never spoke yesterday,
rudely mute it was and brown.
A palm touched my shoulder
to remind me - I was alone.
How the water arches like a serpent,
how lurid the dreaming waters,
rudely waked,
petals never again white.
Why does the water speak
and not the grass?
At least the palm moves,
looms.

Falling

fall, lover falling
you are a soft leaving
like the gentle, unnoticed slipping
of lover leaves from autumn branches
      seeming strength in spring
      brittle and breaking
      grieving in winter
            but a crystal kiss
            white soft
            and leaving
            permeates the earth

The Beeches

The days I studied every tree
I knew them more by reputation
than by their name or occupation,
the job their wood is used to fill.
Now time has taught that beech are best
as homes for squirrels or signs to mark
a boy's way home as woods grow dark.
The old trees die from inside out
and form a hollow hulk to warm
the lives they house. The wood that is lost
the beetles take, and birds in turn.
And so their use for boards and beams
is limited, except the few
the loggers take for pulp and crates.
The giants are scarred where the woodpecker worked
and where I carved essential facts
in jackknife script so long ago.
For beeches were best for dates and hearts
that carry me back on woodland walks
and tell me the marks the beeches made on me
are deeper yet than those I went to see.

Space Mountain

A roller coaster is quite
a two edged thing
and like all modern things
is good and bad.

It demonstrates
the ups and downs of life
and is most blunt in speech
to those who ride the thing,
just hear the children screech.

But as we must face up to fear
or fear will surely rule us,
it is not all a wicked thing.

Somewhere in that blackened time
we were face to face with evil
but the good of it was,
as all must end,
when it did,
we both knew heaven -
a thankful prayer for the good in men
and spit in the eye of the devil.

The Spring

I traveled farther in than out
to find the spring I speak about;
and still I wonder if it flows
as first I watched it when it rose.
But why I dug for a day, then two,
with all the world quite out of view
was just to delve a mystery;
the spring I knew was just a key.
I was a city boy at play
held out from all the yesterday
of knowledge that could help me now
to capture sustenance from soil.
The strangest ferns and aspen trees
yet whispered with an ancient breeze
translated by a spirit guide,
from dampened earth to add a clue
and prints of animals who knew
that there was water hidden here.
And so without machine or witch
I marked my spot and laid a ditch
like some new Moses of the sod
with faith in where I struck my rod.
And there I dug, nor did I doubt,
that I would find the water out.
And when the spring began to flow
with clearest water cold as snow,
I cried aloud that all might see
my labor's new found destiny
in water brimming up to show
to anyone who did not know -

just listen to the Earth's reply
when thirst is great and lips are dry.

The Day the Big Tree Fell

I completely missed
the day the big tree fell.

I thought its roots
went down to hell.

I was at college,
a man almost,
and was amazed to hear
it only broke a fence
and a plum tree.

It didn't reach the house,
and it didn't reach me.

The Reckoning

The days of youth are long in leisure;
it then was easy to neglect
the duties that in retrospect
become the measure of a man.
I'd leave my job half done at noon
to check the meadows, creeks and hills
and often I would stay too late,
nor think of food upon my plate
while I was figuring the will
that caused an indigent daffodil
to bloom among the ferns and vines
so far in time from human kind.
Whose ancestor had passed this way
and planted flowers as if to stay
and was that all he left behind?
Oh, I knew of a fire that scorched the brick
and melted glass that lay beneath
the old frame house where supper waited.
I knew we had built on his foundation
to try and work out our salvation
without much thought to when or where
he laid his flowers out with care.
But a man's youth is only a page
and a man's dream in a different age
is harder to reckon that why a boy
stays late in the wood to merely enjoy
a few yellow blooms he would pick for his mother
or a few yellow questions he would save for another.

The Medicine Bug

I often dreamed the wilderness
wonderfully strange.
So when I finally saw the western range,
I felt I'd seen it all before
in mountains where the eagle soared
and miles of ancient ocean floor
were condemned to dry.
There in dusty desert
sailed the sulfur yellow butterfly.
They were obscure and inscrutable
to those who modern
used the land in plunder
from its quiet repose.
Once men knew their meaning
and their joy so,
that they would draw
the reins of the travois
to silence other sounds
to hear the message.
The language of the butterfly was clear,
as it arose to signal
them to camp,
for here was fire's
protection from the damp
and here were fish
and antelope and deer,
the medicine for still another year.
And so I called the insect
by their names, the medicine bug
of Creek, and Crow and Plains.

Raintree

Besides the fact my father
always wished to grow one
far above its temperate range,
I always wondered why the raintree
held my fascination so.
A modest tree in size,
not particularly beautiful,
it is drab for most of a year.
Yet in fall the yellow blooms
consume last year's memory,
and imbue the sky and earth
with flowers live and dying.
Like a fragrant snow,
a saffron tenderness
kisses the earth beneath
the homely branches.
The tree grows large
in beauty only,
unlike the movie giant
where metaphor of size
misstates majesty.
And as the weeks go by,
the falling blooms transform
to russet parchment pods
that rustle and whisper
in the breeze
and house the seeds
for future generations.
Perhaps my father knew
that in the fall the raintree

claims two final shows,
a yellow fevered symphony
then fades to bittersweet
and blushing hopefulness.

A Villanelle 1969

Spring comes on quickly and blossoms too soon
and the season that's truest is the season that's near.
Summer brings death in the first days of June.

The blooms that now linger do not linger at noon,
the blossoms then shrivel and shutter in fear
for Spring comes on quickly and blossoms too soon.

The lushness is too soon converted to dune,
the coolness is too soon converted to sear,
and Summer brings death in the first days of June.

The Spring is a time to soak in the moon,
the blossoms are perishing, embrace them and hear
that Spring comes on quickly and blossoms too soon.

This frail space is truest and truly a boon
and Spring is the time to caress for it's clear
that Summer brings death in the first days of June.

The Summer is dry and staunch as the tomb
where Springtime is wetness so gaudy and dear,
it comes on too quickly and blossoms too soon
then Summer brings death in the first days of June.

Meadow

a greening meadow waits
and breathless yearns
for us to come to her
and touch the edges
of her comfort
with startled looks
to left and right
and she, being
a lover herself
will shyly laugh
as birds curiously
tip their heads
and a warm rush
of summer wind
shall take us
as the grass is parted

Contrast

The winter sun breaks through
my window after rain
and makes a solid beam in blue
of cigarettes I smoked
in waiting out the storm.
I thought the wall would need a brace
to bear against the race of light.
The sun is keenest after gloom
of rainy winter afternoons.

A Tattered Hat

This ragged hat
with tatters front and rear
has eyes that cannot see
and on its mouth
no lips glisten.
I found it in a cabin
in the spring of '68.
It cannot say
so I surmise -
a hobo left it there
next to his gin bottle.
He got it from
a banker gentlemen
for cleaning out his
garbage cans.
A tailor nearly
took it home for his
but settled on a derby.
Once it fell into
the lake and I saved
it from a weedy death.
I hope its next companion
realizes how benign
a world it is
has not yet cast
this hat aside.

Bantam Roosters and Pleasure Boosters

I knew a man who had too many friends,
small use they were but so he did pretend
and drink with them at night like men who sense
that life should yield much more than mere pretense.

He raised a farm of bantam chicks and roosters
that seemed to him a flock of morale boosters.
The males were bright and beautiful and vain;
the useless hens ranged free and were a bane.

His wife could never seem to understand
the use of bantams nesting in the sand.
They never used the nests that were prepared
though bated with Good Friday eggs and prayered.

She never understood the friends at all
or why he did not come to supper's call.
She could not see the use of bantam roosters
and she did not feel the need for pleasure boosters.

Yet Another Love Poem

Were this night shared with you
the cold would not intrude.
And if your ears could hear,
this monotonous grumbling
of a sleepy city would become
a source of wonder.
If your lips touched mine,
the night would fold around us like satin
and frightening sounds would become
an anxious breath in the dawn.

Unheard

The music of monotonous midnight
is a strange and rhythmic drumming.
It beats like some great machine
unheard because it was always there.
Like some mad bird
straining to break its tether,
it is the pulse and strain
of an imagined medley
that plays with memory.
It makes the music mute,
it gives freedom to silence,
it ties the music down.

Black Widow

I watched a spider climb a wall,
I watched her crawl down again
and voices whispered for a call,
that's all there is for men.
I sit and watch the day go up
and watch the clock go down,
it seems my blood runs down a rut
to oceans without sound.
The spider climbed to find a fly,
crawled down to stop and think
and wonder that a day went by
to end in sunset pink.
You are a lucky one I said,
small thoughts - no joy, no dread.
But then I saw beneath a leg
a simple trace of red,
an hourglass that did not beg.
I knew she did not care to know
her sun was going down.
She raised her back as if to show
defenses that were sound.
But I was cursed a larger brain
that knows no sting of man
can stay a day from its decline
or give him greater span.

Pet

There's no one around
and the cat won't complain
if I open the window
and let in the rain.

The cat doesn't care
if I sit here and stare.
No, me and the cat,
we like it like that.

I can sleep in the day
and think in the night
and the cat doesn't worry
what's wrong or what's right.

There's no one to say
that my tuna fish salad
isn't spicy enough
or limpid or pallid,
to add mayonnaise
or improve on my ways.

And me and the cat,
we like it like that.

Two Rocks

The creek in the wood
behind my childhood home
was rich
with the entertainment
of questioning.
What were
just two rocks
to some
to me seemed to hide
eternal mysteries.

Most rocks that I dragged home
had found a final resting place
upon that creek bed
where water washed them
each and every day
and kept them shining
like jewels is a rare display.

But now and then
the anthropologist of spring,
behind a plow,
would dredge up from the soil
a clay caked shard of ancient stone.

And that was cause enough
to pause a while
and wonder who had cast it there,
or had some great upheaval
of the strata

rolled it to this spot
never till now
to be touched
by curiosity
or washed
by rain.

Weakness

beautiful
and girlish women
always were
a weakness for me
liquid
and tender
dark eyes
seeking out a life
needing help
with no betrayal
not so different
from me

The Voice in the Wood

In summer I could hear
the voice in the wood
when the wood was alive
with slithering confusion
and life was a hot green blur
as the creek ran rushes.
In winter the murmurs
of forgotten echoes call me
to a childhood bridge,
a bridge to dreaming.
A final silent day
before the spring
when the voice commands
an ultimate act of faith,
I flirt with denial.
But quite accidentally,
the elocution of returning birds,
the flat statement of green tongues.

I have grown familiar with broken things,
the despondent and the desperate
and I have wandered in tangled mazes
rich with mocking disappointment
for the bogus gold of spring.
And I have picked the rusted heap
searching for a bit of color,
listening for a rustling,
an affirmation of life.
I have felt the sharpened edge
of unrequited aspiration

and I have been amazed
to see the throng mirrored
in a shattered shard of looking glass.

Here I sit, retired of hearing
old truths reiterated
from un-inquisitive oracles.
Here I receive,
unabashed and without bias,
the tenable with the probable,
the unuttered undeniable,
the randomness
of inspiration.
Here I affirm the voice
regardless of school,
regardless of intention
and beyond misconception.
Here I assert un-banished survival.

The voice babbled
like a young creek
in a hurry to grow with rivers.
It spoke confused truths
and non-confusing lies.
It laid down hot and cold
explaining creation in fairy tales.
It was a kind voice,
substantial in tone,
reassured and reassuring.
It was the voice of functional rule.
It spoke only to point onward.

Gray air of dawn
pierced by a natal moon
broken by the whispering wisdom
of a child's question.

Deep was the wood and deep
its rhapsodies without danger.
Beasts as large as houses roamed,
silver mansions reigned
and clear water flowed.
Among the hills with holy names,
beneath the eagle's beech,
a secret lake, and filled with love,
eluded me by day for only dreams
could show the way.
Those were the free times
before the voice began
to warn of the end of dreams,
of the time the dreams are real.

I fell to my knees
and spoke with sacred forces
making timid pleas
for undisputed phrases
or in their stead a peaceful place
to lay my head.
I was answered
by a non-committal breeze.

There with wonder did I walk
and there with laughter did I seek
and there with ignorance did hear

all vindicated dreams and fear.

The voice never ceased,
it trickled and roared like the tide,
it drew me farther in,
it pushed me out
to test the gold of spring.
It demanded answers
from speculation.
It demanded choices
from induction.
It wet me down,
it dried me out,
it made me think,
it made me doubt.

Then rippled in the waters
a human halo, a blessing
essential as dew
dawning a quiet pond.
The voice proclaimed
the consecration of a man.

I believed the voice.
I loved, I gave and got,
I lost and was resigned.
And the trial
was a trial of existence,
of hot and cold,
of wet spring nights
and dry winter days,
was a trial of strength,

of mind and muscle
against life's tendency
for torment.

I played with dreams
and the voice played
with memory.
And I played with thoughts
like notions from rare books
and I sailed my toy boat,
pieced together chanciness
in the storm.

Then did the voice crack
with age and a vision
of the damned.
Then did I see the
cracked wisdom of
the world and death.
Then did the voice
roar like a winter river
beneath a lost bridge
to nothingness.
It washed me
in the wisdom
of despair.

Death is worth life
the voice rattled -
it comes.
Strive not for death,
it comes and the voice

of what was will cease
to the gasping cries
of a new age.
Search not for death
and the wood
is a constant symphony.

Old Dust

The smell of old folks houses
makes me think
that men <u>are</u> made of dust.
When I was young we used to go
by fifteen miles of lonely road
to see the old ones on the home place.
I did not know the meaning then
of musty odors there
and thought them just too old to clean
or too far gone to care.
But I chanced upon my home
one winter day and noticed there
reminders of the fate we all must bear.
It is a mix of dust and home,
precursors of totemic tombs.

Old Man

Death is patient waiting
to this old man
who gazes in the park
as in a vain attempt to spark
awareness of the motive
that brought him here.

He cannot move his mind
but vaguely knows
it has to do with spring
and laughter.

He has confused
the flowers in his path
with girls in rowboats
smiling at their lovers.

He shakes his head
and only for a moment
his eyes return to youth.

He passes by a couple
on a bench
and tips his hat
to say the day is good.

Ending Vietnam

Repentance when it comes
never fails to drown the sound
of roaring guns.
        But none
        save the sun
        can make raindrops
        or wildflowers.
No new made
garden wall,
no medicinal bower
injected in the soul
can silence the cries
or drug the indignation.
        Forgive, forgive,
        and sound it till
        the lungs are dry,
        but not one blast
        will be revoked
        and not one soul
        will be evoked.
A great waterfall
mingling with the blood
of the fallen
bleaches the stain
and roars louder
than the grief and pain.
        A greater and much
        different plot
        is planned,
        oxidizing law and land.

Poetry #28

Poetry does not sing songs.
It sadly lacks harmonic words
to merely mock the vibrant birds.
Music is a longing
removed from living,
a secret place
of metered giving.
Music and song
are man's long longing
for transcendent wings.
In birds the music glides
in quarter notes
and full harmonic.
So there abides
in only feathered things
songs that rise
on rhythmic wings.

Firefly '66

moon, stars and fireflies
the moon is new
the stars are dim with mist
a firefly is blinking in the wet darkness
brighter than the moon and stars
an instant and gone
a star fading
lost in the universe

Aboriginal

Essential man
is clad in green
and dew of dawn,
his drink,
is held in crystal fruit.
The song he hears
is only played
on an imagined lute.
He takes from Earth
but what he must
and treats it as
a sacred trust.
He makes a melody sublime,
intoxicant surpassing wine.

Elusive Meanings

does the forest tremble
realizing the alienation of roots
the isolation of leaf and vine
or does the wind
without meaning
make a rustling in the fall
a chaotic breath
that touches all

A Space Between

There is no need
to feel the flame
to know
that there is heat.

There is no need
to touch the sea
or put it to my lips
to know its briny nature.

I know great mysteries
by the merest hint.

Life and death
are close companions
separated only by sensation.

I cannot see the roots
of my beginning.

I cannot smell
the smoke of autumn.

Yet I am acquainted
with a space between
as a man of middle years
knows young children
and old dogs.

The Long Way Home from Indian River

There is a distance to my home,
not half the road behind me.
Yet I sit and watch
the sun go down on Indian River.
My food and beer are done
and still I stare at quiet water,
green ripples of sea grass
and tailing redfish.
I could retreat the sooner,
my cooling motorcycle
waits to take me
back to my beginnings.
I might then gain
familiar rest
before the darkness
settles in.
Yet with sunset fading,
I hold to this encounter:
a piece of the horizon,
a portion of the sunset,
a beaker of the night.
Would I return the shorter way,
omit circuitous wandering,
an easy road I'd find
but I must choose
the stranger route
and unfamiliar pleasure,
solitude in afterglow,
discreet,
sequestered treasure.

Brave Blooms

Precocious blooms
ignore the cold
and boldly
in the spring unfold
while just this day
I lit the fire
to warm salvation
and desire.
My northern days
have taught me sure
that scarlet blooms
provide no cure
for emptiness
and excess pain
and piercing days
of bleak spring rain.
They are a gesture
for the sight,
they know not when
the time is right
but bloom the same
on the happenstance
that spring will stay;
they take a chance.

Deep Sleep

A sailor dreams
upon the deck
of all the places
he has been,
of Turkish baths,
the land of Moors
and all the storied
foreign shores.
He does not see
me on the dock
both out of sight
and sound.
The air is buzzing
all around
with old world ports
and oriental visions.
And though in sleep
a peace he found,
I would not close the door.
I thought no ill to fill desire,
no harm to silently inquire
upon a dreamers sleep.
The sailor dreamed
upon the deck
and turning in his sleep,
I saw the water at his side,
I never knew how deep.

Royalty of Night

When darkness falls and shadows flee
and colors take a somber tone,
I know the force that sets men free
I see it in the violet of dusk.

The sky of noon was newborn blue
but now it takes a bishops hue
and struggles imperially
with the red sunset till purple falls.

The sky is coronate with rays of light
and though it soon casts off its robe
and sets aside the crown of day
yet never does it forsake its majesty.

Content, the king of evening reigns
but for a moment in glowing flame
till night impeaches rule of day
and the dark nocturnal dominion
is free to cast its diamonds in the sky.

Love's Precedence

What love proclaims,
spring cannot outdo in eloquence.
Love is the poetry
of man's greatest gift.
We feel the sadness in a sunset.
We weep like no animal can.
Standing upright,
we embrace to the very soul.
No words can frame
substantiation of love's claim.
Spring's gusty boasts of bloom
cannot surpass the blush of love
for love is beyond the essence of a sunset,
and more remote a jewel than starlight.
Love is iridescent, elusive, gleaming.
Love is indulgent, dreaming.
We are compelled to it
like some addiction.
It is a mad rush
of euphoria lovers feel.
It is a state that words
cannot describe,
all feelings throbbing
to a teenage beat.
It is a rush denying speech,
denying spring of any claim
to consecrate the world,
denying and yet affirming,
a pulse, a gesture signifying
love's precedence.

Inspiration

Air to breathe
and fuel the soul
a fire within
a rhythm
a drum pounding
divinity
a god who cares
and if there be
a heartbeat
close at hand
a person
someone to believe in
someone to believe in you
arms
lips
soft eyes
breathless wanting

Short Creek Valley

I've often said that I grew up
in a boyhood's perfect paradise
and here's a little bit of evidence.
If paradise has a water source,
Short Creek is a worthy one
with water clear as a summer breeze
after rain, potable, in the upper valley.
I often thought when I was young
that Short Creek was an ironic name,
my expeditions ran deep into the hills
but never reached the source.
Short Creek was long in life's lessons
and longer yet in memories.
In age we all say things shrink.
The childhood farm is no longer huge,
the creek was truly not so long,
though still I would not call it short
for it was formidable.
Perhaps that was the first lesson,
living in a confusing world
so soon to be a shrinking village -
the world is full of contradiction.

I fished Short Creek
from its mouth at the muddy Yazoo
and well into the hills.
Catfish lurked there and alligator gar,
sunfish, bass, soft-shell and green turtles
and wayward wood duck strays
that overflew the nearby Horseshoe Lake.

It was easy to imagine then
the native ancestry of the land -
the Cherokee and Choctaw,
the ancient Yazoo tribesman
standing in a dugout made of cypress
as he polled his way
across the flat land delta strip
before the hills turned bayou to rapids.
Then, abundant deer, bear and turkey
roamed the land.
In hills above the valley,
the Indians made their camps
and shards and arrow heads
were turned behind our plows
and taught that treasure,
that life itself,
comes from the earth
and that man returns to it.
That was the second lesson.

The third lesson was about wonder
and joy and faith in intuition.
The creek was a playground
in my childhood time:
a place for skipping rocks,
a place to camp, to swim,
to split a first beer with a buddy,
a place of muddy banks
to form a water slide,
a diving platform for the fool hardy,
sand beaches that rival Cancun,
a place to spy on skinny dippers

and find what girls were all about,
a holy balm to consecrate a friendship.
Yes, Short Creek was a playground
but also a place of higher learning:
a place to explore the crux of living,
to wonder and to find
what was,
what is,
and what was yet to be.

Wind Words

Late night's low song is a wind word
humming an infinite sailor's tune,
beneath the sails, beneath the moon.

Below the waters, unheard,
ripples mask the quiet sky
and only we can sense
a presence
turning from the lee,
a storm tossed sea.

The wind words whisper
secret sounds to drowsy ears,
a stirring in the air, a murmur
before the first stroke of fire.

The Old Voice

My veteran voice is cracked and dry,
the end I fear is drawing near
and nothing left is truly dear,
I can forsake all alibi.

I cannot sing, I cannot dance.
Who used to be the instigator
is now a folding chair spectator
who will not take a vocal chance.

Is life a sing song forced repeating
of melodies I failed to learn
as memories forever burn
like soldier harmonies retreating?

I notice old men still can hum,
a mantra and a winking eye
a vagrant notion then a sigh
a nod to measures known as wisdom.

Still I'd prefer a second chance
at youthful, awkward song and dance.

The Magic Store

Near the edge of town
was the county poor house
the abode of local poverty
and unfortunate birth.

Blind Lonzo, the town's
blind beggar stayed there.

From the poor house,
it was two miles to town,
one more to the Magic Store.

Lonzo would walk it every Saturday.

That's when I worked at the Magic Store.

I knew he was proud so I always
allowed him to pay a bit.

But he wasn't so dumb and one day he
turned to me and smiled and said,
"My Gawd, ten cent fo' a loaf a bread:
dis sho' is a Magic Sto'."

Dying Green

As I walked from the wood
the palest dogwood
ever seen
trailed out its life.

As I walked from the wood
no lover's breath
could cause a blush to pause
upon the blossoms.

As I walked from the wood
the trees were faint with dying green
and love could not be seen.

Trigonometry

I am tired of pacing
tired of chasing
life away from the eyelids
with backhand swipes
still memory buzzes
like a noxious fly
I try to walk away
I try but cannot
get the hang
of tangential functions

Better Than Coffee

I hear the dawn's first bird;
has love returned to me
or will I sleep ere long
with only memories
and greet the silent day
to empty arms?
The night bird sings
the way I feel,
so glad the sun will rise.
But now my lady sleeps
and does not hear my sighs.
I wake her with a kiss,
to let her hear the song
that she might take the risk
to stay the morning long.

Rodeo

the best and brightest boots
to aid an eagle stride
that soars above the crowd
with silver spangles
on his shirt
I see the animals
breath of hate and fear
the wind whirs
and the sky bleeds

Indian Summer

something
from the spring
that keeps us going
that clears the winter sky
and coaxes deceived buds
and doomed butterflies
to taste the bogus season
sends men out for reckoning
tired of contemplating walls
a yearning instinct
pent up
frozen desire
and mixed
with a toast to memory
the touch of a gentle hand
the hope for bluer skies
a lover's sigh
before the pretense dies

The Rare Vice

To know a man but by his verse
is knowing him at best and worst
like knowledge that we have of men
known chiefly for their major sin.
There's no other sin like poetry
since Adam's lusty apple tree.
Poetry was long a vice
in brothels of the cheapest price
and yet the sages cannot say
that verse has always been that way.
But value in a modern rhyme
is never worth the thinnest dime.
So getting on to men and verse
let me tell you of the curse.
A simple thought that you might think
I must not fail to print ink
though is be noon by light of day
the middle of the month of May
or though it's two A.M. or four
when snow piles up against the door.
And yet I write and take abuse
and jot my lines of little use.
To know a man but by his sin
is knowing him as one in ten.

The Spoiling of the Devil's Garden

The hint of life in spring,
the newest buds
that died all winter long,
must have thought
all nature grieving,
lost from hope
in fear and cold
and loneliness.
The hint of life,
the thawing brittle sleep
curls out an arm,
a golden finger sprout
foretells a wrinkled hand
to consecrate a greening life
and promises of things to come.
Five months of death a year
would seem enough.
Periodic bloom,
perennial doom,
suffice for them,
a momentary tomb.
The hint of life in spring
proclaims that we endure;
and still men's eyes
must register surprise.

Enclosures

The wall before me now is white
but should I choose to quit the light
the wall dissolves in shades of gray.
And if I choose to sleep all day
and never build the wall again
and never paint the sun again
and never call the colors back
the wall is then but vacuum black.
The white wall of my pensive room
abruptly ends the day.
The spiral to a waiting tomb
distinctly walls the way.

The Trouble

Pity I wasn't asked to speak
before God spent His famous week.
I'd not have held the apple back
or dealt the snake a mighty whack.
If those reforms were not enough,
I'd sure have called the devil's bluff,
perhaps forgave Eve's indiscretion
with absolution and confession.

No Wings

A random cawing jay,
a trilling redbird
calling for its mate,
cannot endow
the sibilance
of a spring breeze
with the murmur
of a lover's breath.
They are a small adjunct
to foolish fragile wings,
the many colored
muteness of butterflies.
They flee with balmy idle awe
at my indifferent pshaw.
These wings can never compensate
for what I know of love and fate.
Love leaves in fall,
windblown, with no voice
to populate the cold of winter,
to give wing to springtime,
to hold me longer in the Earth
or raise me much above my birth.

Raven Riddle

Sable child of fantasy,
you never rode a natal wave,
you never suckled human flesh,
you slept within and black without
and wondered at the world about you.
And yet you wondered not at all
resting in a bottle by the wall.
Darkness born upon a page,
a saving breath upon my age.
All of flashing sloe eyed beauty,
feminine, naked,
no regret,
ebony body,
hair of jet.
When knowing too much
won't let me rest
but I would sooner
lie awake
than die,
raven dreams to set me free,
dark paragon of ecstasy.

Pangean Fantasy

Continents of experience separate us
and no Pangea embraces mankind.
Can we reach for the horizon
and behold a brother there?
Can we look with hopeful eyes,
and find transcendence,
a longing for pacific dreams,
archetypal visions,
a time when oceans were rivers,
an inconvenient blue divide
between tribes of single lineage?

Some men still dream a bigger dream,
and now and then will nominate salvation
to be voted on in beer halls, bedrooms
and breakfast meetings.
Now and then a bigger dreamer steps up
against the naysayers and money mongers,
against hatred, favoring love,
the long house and the harvest table.

Another hand reaches out for redemption,
a millennial tide of doubt and fear pulls it down
and threatens half of what we are
or could become.
Can touch heal, can muscle work in unison,
can the only enemies
be known as pain, hunger,
loneliness, greed and cruelty?
Pangea waits, the continents are moving.

Dream Beat

In dreams, the soft exhale
of affection, the friendship
in a greeting hug
melts in trembling alto tones
to a lover's sigh that whispers –
hold me.
In dreams, the punishment
of almost intimacy
in a cousin like kiss
fades to song as enticing eyes
and an upturned chin
invite a kiss,
silently submerged
from atmosphere.
The melody I hear is a fantasy in blue,
a gentle minor key,
until, like an old song,
she leads me by the hand
to secret places bright
with the clash of cymbals.
The hot jazz of appetite
is for ecstasy in her arms.
The longing in the soul,
the harmony, is for the afterglow,
the cooling back-beat of drumming brushes,
the embrace of eyes fixed on one another,
the skin on skin,
and for the moment,
no pain in the universe.

Fragmentary Blues

the music dies and smolders
like the embers of a lost fire
the symphony of day
ends with cooler oboe sounds
viola and kettle drum
the eyes close calmed by fantasy
heat endures only as memory
memory of winged desire
a moment and lost
in evening's cold and careless breeze
the dream was real
seagulls soared on thermal
springs of air
the dream was dream
the heat the crescendo
brass and violin
chilled by the somber moan
of the reeds
we seek and waves
of harmony break
we pray and wells of silence call
and in the end
a cawing sound
punctuates
a foolish hollow plea
seagulls in a blue white sky
searching unhurried
greedy but blameless
searching mindlessly
for the noon day meal

Mare Sirenum

darkest lunar isle
so beautiful the song
remote
alluring
fantastic
an hypnotic call
that ever lures men
to chemistry of loneliness

expanse of silver
tarnished
with elusive dreams
desire
a noble illusion
a plutonian glow
remote
unreal
a fragmentary rock

a siren's tune
emboldens youth
with oceanic vision
but all of time
bestows on age
an earthbound
tender wisdom
for tethered dreams
and lower orbits
an earnest kiss to silence
archetypal memory

Cat Dreams

are cat dreams a curse
to those born of Leo
or are they just
a bitter gift of age
caged symbols
of center ring losses
the betrayal of cat dreams
is clear
I crack my whip
and shout denial
but desire pays no heed
a slinking feline
a chestnut panther
challenges my sleeping brain
with sibilant vibrato sighs
and will not quit the ring
I want no dream
they have all abandoned me
I want not and yet I do want
I want this purring dream to stay
but no one knows like me
that dreams deceive
and only death is true
in time the sleep will come
when all the circus spectacle is done
the cats will sleep in their boxes
and I in mine
where dreams unravel
along with all my tears
like play worn balls of yarn
and cat dream fears

Panic 2 A.M.

when I think of all the stories
I have heard the travelers tell
I know all there is of heaven
I know all I need of hell

but I believe I see the ending
you know a storm is coming soon
that old willow tree is bending
I hear a wildcat's angry howl

elusive sleep is just an eyeball
glowing red into the gloom
hopeless shadows spin a nightmare
softly creeping to my room

after midnight lurks a power
beyond the pale of grace or sin
it's a brooding evil hour
I call it panic 2 A.M.

I am caught up in a cyclone
too much pain and emptiness
my brain is whirling caught in exile
a dark vortex of loneliness

did that hand I held a moment
traveling on the road to glory
ever know I heard their tale
ever hear my own sad story

it is late at night and calling
is the wildcat's lonely growl
night time shadows surely falling
the cat is answered by the owl

after midnight lurks a power
beyond the pale of grace or sin
it's a brooding evil hour
I call it panic 2 A.M.

every man is just an island
whirlpool eddies guard the reef
hungry dragons by the wayside
forked tongues and no relief

I know the hurricane is coming
lizard fire to burn the earth
storm cloud thunder distant drumming
fire and ice and no rebirth

the gyre will churn the muddy water
eye wall screams and anvil sounds
the wild cat cowers in an alley
a rumbling wave throughout the town

after midnight lurks a power
beyond the pale of grace or sin
it's a brooding evil hour
I call it panic 2 A.M.

memories' colors all are fading
wind whipped rags upon a line
hail and lightning now retreating
like the windstorm in my mind

the wildcat's track has all but vanished
the owl is nowhere to be seen
the lizards lick their tongues and wonder
was mankind a futile dream

the stories idiots must tell us
of life's glory and it's pain
recycle with galactic nova
the wanton cities of the plain

after midnight lurks a power
beyond the pale of grace or sin
it's a brooding evil hour
I call it panic 2 A.M.

Youth and Age

youth
is a wild adventure
the strangest mix
of confidence
and doubt
age steals
all but confidence
and plays with that
a cat and mouse game
I look across a room
and a wild impulse
glances my way
crashing doubt
intrudes
confidence fades
only a dying wish
remains
memory and desire
mixed
mixed up
with the fog of yesterday
the blur of victory
blind loss
lost poetry
a moonlight dance
a tear
a regret
and
disappearing sand
framed by a mournful
singular silhouette

Dragon Slayer

before the closing act is done
and if a crowning wish is won

before the utmost prayer I pray
just one more dragon might I slay

and save a lady in distress
perhaps to win a brief caress

for what is all of life about
unless a man can have some clout

and yet in age the sword must fail
and knightly muscles must grow frail

desire forever knows no bounds
and so with memory's arms surrounds

her beauty for a dreamer's sleep
distinctly I forever keep

till dragons find eternal rest
and knights all end their final quest

Some are not Loved

some are not loved
some are lost
lost souls
caught up
in a bad roll
in craps
a cliché too real
for the street to hide

down that street
turning in blind alleyways
the quiet and desperate ones
hide from the light
and place their bets

the careless universe
turns its head and laughs
for the joke of age
of illness
of poverty
and ignorance

some are not loved
proof to one
of god's snickering jest
rolling the dice
making some hard point
in a game
no one wins
and no one
understands

an old man's hands

a turn of cards
an old man's hands
to frame a prayer
in memory's eyes
the final ace
some withered hope
that life is not
a sad remembrance
of winning hands or lost
this old man's hands
with innocence
reach out to place a bet
a hope filled blessing
to the mirror of youth
I look upon these hands
have loved and lost
nurtured
cherished
chided
pleaded
past
age
these old man's hands
still linger
still hold a wish
a flush in hearts
ace high
enduring luck
a final royal desire
a moment
a chance

hermit

loneliness
is the cost
of frail protection
a hermit's way
is safely to observe
and not participate
despair
is a quiet retreat
a reassuring lover
an ease
no strife
no striving
love is a foolish child
busy
with knowing nothing
of night
a candle
that dies a bit
with every hour
of its expression
silence and raindrops
are a ticking clock
a dark river
runs through it all
and down
to a boundless
universal
and gods are content
in their isolation
for they know
not pain

Sunrise, Sunset

I have always preferred sunsets
but lately long for the sunrise.
Now I am left with faded memories
of the dawn, the building light,
the promise of almost and wishes.
Strange that the same colors abide
at birth or death.
Crimson desire, purple solitude,
russet and rose regret,
all girl pink, baby boy blue
and the bluing gray of aged ships.
Age does not eliminate desire,
it only fans tangerine embers with a breeze
that wakes remembrance of wanting.
Majestic colors of failure haunt memory
for even kings must die alone.
Death's jester is a parody
of purple audacity.
The reds are the worst,
sodden tears, the cowering,
the crowded ruse of wasted,
wanting, dreaming, mistaken starts.
Sunrise is a girlish thing,
lace concealed pink secrets,
soft arms and shelter,
a port for the war weary,
the battle worn,
until tomorrow comes.

Clint's Grief

Why must poets bleed
for the empty ache
of lost love, of lost youth,
the wickedness of death
and the dying
pain of distance in time,
the agony of memories.
My tears are for the weight
of all unending grief,
for the silent inner war,
and for all brutality
of nations and of men.
I weep for the shame,
the endurance of hate,
the frailty of caring.
It is a ripping knife
that tears a heart
and kills the soul
with no savior to redeem.
Planets whirl, moonbeams fall
and evil creeps
like a stalking maniac
that knows no joy.
There is no armor,
the monster comes,
hooded and red eyed
in the terrible night.
Speechless is my pain,
no tongue to speak the loss,
my love, my hope, my faith,
my peace, my soul, my life.

Boundary Values

no longer rich
was the man
who told me yesterday
that had I not known riches
I would not understand
the pain
to reach the top
and then to lose it all
yet all he lost was cash
but yet I pitied him
and wondered had he known
a sweeter
vanished treasure
the silent company
of eyes and hearts
so interlocked
one could not tell
where one began
and where the other
ceased
I could not laugh
nor tell him truly
could not belittle
petty gambling losses
but thought him poorer still
who valued money so
that empty was his heart
he had not lost a love
but surely never had
he loved
and so had lost it all

Things I Like

I like the bachelor pad
my favorite colors
tan and blue
political incorrectness
inappropriate clothing
an open collar
and an open schedule
I like dogs
hounds especially
small rivers
and small boats
I like cooking in a skillet
Dutch oven stew for company
I like not worrying
about cholesterol
the economy
the wars
or anything else
I like hot weather
orchids
all flowers
pretty women
birds
the beach with no one there
red wine is good
sunset
wind in the pine trees
memories
silence
a moment to think
a moment to not think

Need

poems of age
need no punctuation
no rhythm
no irascible rhyme
no reason

surely
a self indulgent frost
falls in the fall
and informs

as the end approaches
what will be
supersedes what was

the meaning of sacrifice
comes clear

the coldness comes
the deeds are done

we stand alone
before a careless universe
and wish but well
to those who will not grieve
our passing long
as rest
at last
comforts need

Sparkle's Victory

I know but one
among us common folk
has earned the name Sparkle.
She brings a smile and hope
with only a look.

When Sparkle is sad
we all are sad.
When she laughs,
we all laugh.

I am not sure
from which planet
she emanates.
Not from the dull Earth.

A world of diamond
and starlight there must be,
a Tinkerbelle home
that makes us want to believe.

And when Sparkle loses
we all lose.
And when she wins,
we all know victory.

I Dream in Poetry

I dream in poetry
and all the colors of autumn.
My days are haunted with nuance,
the insinuation of a mockingbird,
hot luscious sun on my face,
the flash of wet, feminine eyes.

A day in thirds is music.
Morning tunes the day,
then statutory noon
utters its cantations
till a liquid violin sunset
weeps with passion's colors.

I dreamed in spring
and green gold promise
was a betrayal of hope.

Summer has gone,
lost lilies drop their seed
before the cold wind turns.
I dream in poetry
and all the colors of autumn.
Forgotten songs echo hot nights
and memory's kiss.
The music has died.
Blind day gives way
to dreams of falling leaves,
and softest night
to carry them away.

Emmy's Legacy

Once upon a time,
there was a boy named Harry
who dreamed.
Harry would tell you,
he had a friend named Emmy,
a lavender dinosaur, seven feet tall.
Everywhere that Harry went, Emmy went.
His parents said it was only his imagination.
But Harry knew Emmy was real.
As Harry grew up,
he still talked about Emmy to his friends,
but failed to say she was a dinosaur
or speak of her beautiful color.
But Emmy was always with him.
Through the ups and downs,
sharing the joy,
grieving the losses.
Emmy was a great comfort
as Harry grew old.
And near the end
Harry shared with me
his secret.
Harry and Emmy died on the same day.
But Harry left to me the greatest gift of all,
Emmy's legacy, the permission to dream.

Ghost Orchid

A few miles south of Eden,
I wandered the primordial garden
in the land of Confederate Trillium,
the now endangered bloom
that flourished in my youth
in the open understory of paradise.
The flora was pre-historic,
singular stands of bamboo
crowded the creek banks.
The riot of the May Apple in Spring
was an intoxicant.
Sovereign fern and mossy streams
were paths to prospects
of grander revelation.
Cocooned silken secrets
in alabaster wrap
waited for the light
while benign serpents mimicked
the ripples of the branch
before the fall of the seasons;
and more remote near Panther Creek
some said the wild cat still patrolled.

Now in age I seek a stranger species,
more elusive than dying memories.
Florida called me south like a Siren's song
and lately dreams command to travel farther,
the Everglades,
the Fakahatchee Strand,
for there the final secret lies.
Beyond all epiphytes,

bromeliads,
royal palms and cypress,
beyond the tannic waters,
the Ghost Orchid is in hiding
but to the less persistent than I.
It is said the wanderer will come upon it,
floating before his eyes ghostlike.
Nearby protectors watch,
necessity of Pond Apple and Pop Ash,
where fixed
by camouflaged roots
the orchid takes its nourishment.
And somewhere in the swamp,
in passion's dance,
the Giant Sphinx Moth searches
for a flash of candent light,
seeks the morning scent of apples.
A panther cries; the indigo snake waits.

Sonnet 47

I wish to find the farthest bloom
that by the seed of rivers rests.
And there in delicate embrace
a rare perfume will be my grace.

Into the mystic glen unguided,
up from the dark and sullen swamp,
I find a garden walled and sided,
the secret keep of mystery's warden.

A light, an ecstasy of breath
beguiles the dream with sweetest scent.
The passion is a christening,
a foil against life's ample torment.

Imagined bloom and far from view,
I seek, but those who find are few.

Far

I am far from home,
far from belief in magic,
from belief in tomorrow.
Foolhardy wishes are vanished.
Maps drawn in the sand
washed away by the tide,
the final leaves of autumn,
fuel no foolish notions
of spring's reprieve.
Sentiments of poetry, art,
paper and stone hopefulness
are betrayals of dreaming.
Tomorrow is a bland sunrise,
no noon day secrets
argue with curiosity,
and an empty
and absurd illusion
frames sundown.
No new season beckons,
only night is left,
cold mystery,
damp velvet darkness -
and until then,
the comfort of defiance.

Index

A Child   63
A Common Situation   69
A Fisherman's Prayer   67
A Space Between   100
A Tattered Hat   83
A Villanelle 1969   81
Aboriginal   99
Above Despair   68
Acceptance   60
Accumulated Defense   51
An Old Man's Hands   131
Bantam Roosters   84
Beginning   12
Better Than Coffee   113
Black Widow   86
Boundary Values   135
Brain Damage   62
Brave Blooms   102
Butterfly Girl   36
Cat Dreams   124
Chain Gang Mississippi   47
Clint's Grief   134
Cold   38
Confrontation   64
Contrast   82
Come up to Dawn   58
D.E.   34
Dawn Leaves   44
Death   19
Deep Sleep   103
Domestic   23

Dragon Slayer   129
Dream   65
Dream Beat   121
Dusty Floors and Open Windows   72
Dying Green   112
Early Seeding   8
Elusive Meanings   99
Emmy's Legacy   140
Enclosures   117
Ending Vietnam   97
Ending   6
Exhaustion   17
Failure to Site Scripture   27
Falling   73
Far   144
Feline   38
Firefly   98
Fragmentary Blues   122
Friend   70
Fruit Fly   54
Ghost Orchid   141
Gift   33
Going On   39
Grassy Key Deer   13
Heat   43
Hermit   132
Hot Dogs and Champaign   36
I Dream in Poetry   139
Incidentals   11
Indian Summer   114
Inspiration   106
Instrumentals   11
Interfacial   73

Jones' Situation   31
Key West Madonna   15
Long Lesson   53
Lost Music   59
Love Poem   44
Love's Precedence   105
Mare Sirenum   123
Meadow   82
Memories of the Seasons   4
Mississippi Mercy   56
Mobile Bay   45
Need   137
No Wings   118
Notion   61
Old Dust   95
Old Man   96
On Leaning Left   30
Pangean Fantasy   120
Panic 2 A.M.   125
Pet   87
Poetry #28   98
Raintree   80
Raven Riddle   119
Recycle   10
Relativity   9
Resignation   42
Rodeo   113
Royalty of Night   104
Rubric   55
Sartartia - Clear Lake Camp   46
Self Defense   50
September Wine   43
Short Creek Valley   107

Silence Sleeps   49
Solitary Concert   58
Some are not Loved   130
Sonnet 37   7
Sonnet 46   11
Sonnet 47   143
Sonnet of Spring   5
Sonnet 39   9
Space Mountain   75
Sparkle's Victory   138
Sun Course   22
Sunrise, Sunset   133
Supernova   21
The Beeches   74
The Children Play   52
The City   17
The County Fair   39
The Cynic   14
The Day the Big Tree Fell   77
The Empty Journal   26
The Final Piece   23
The Fort   40
The Good Doctor   57
The Gravedigger   66
The Greenhouse at Leu Gardens   18
The Introvert   48
The Long Way Home   101
The Magic Store   111
The Medicine Bug
The Old Road   28
The Old Voice   110
The Rare Vice   115
The Reckoning   78

The Spoiling of the Devil's Garden   116
The Spring   76
The Tree House   41
The Trouble   117
The Voice in the Wood   90
Things I Like   136
Thoughts   30
Three Verses on Rhythm   16
Three Nieces   14
Tiger Eye   40
Time   32
Time Piece   19
Trigonometry   112
Twilight's Tow   71
Two Rocks   88
Unheard   85
Values   24
Weakness   89
Wind Words   109
Winter Stand   20
Yet Another Love Poem   85
Youth and Age   128
Youth on the Wing   37

Made in the USA
Charleston, SC
26 December 2010